This Book Belongs To

____

Made in the USA
Las Vegas, NV
27 November 2021

35413267R00068